Celebrations

Louise Spilsbury

W
FRANKLIN WATTS
LONDON · SYDNEY

Franklin Watts
338 Euston Road
London NW1 3BH

Franklin Watts Australia
Level 17/207 Kent Street
Sydney NSW 2000

ISBN 978 1 4451 3040 8
Dewey classification number: 203.6

Series editor: Julia Bird
Art director: Jonathan Hair
Design: Shobha Mucha
Consultant: Joyce Mackley, RE Advisor at RE Today

A CIP catalogue record for this book is available
from the British Library.

Picture credits: Terry J Alcorn/istockphoto: 27tr: Gustavo Andrade/istockphoto:
9tr; Kitch Bain/Shutterstock: 27cl; Annie Griffiths Belt/Corbis: 15br;
Blend Images/Alamy: 11b; Leland Bobbé/Corbis: 6b; Bubbles PL/Alamy: 19b;
Denkon Images/Alamy: 17t; Yvan Dubé/istockphoto: 6t; Simon East/istockphoto:
26t;Laurence Gough/Shutterstock: 15tl; Kirby Hamilton/istockphoto: 9b; Robert
Harding PL/Alamy: 14; Chris Hellier:/Corbis front cover; Moheed Hussain/istockpho-
to: 12t; India Today Group/Getty Images: 13; Rehan Khan/EPA/Corbis: 23b; M A
Pushpa Kumara/EPA/Corbis: 22; Narinda Nanu/AFP/Getty Images: 18;
Nikreates/Alamy: 16t; Crack Palinggi/Reuters/Corbis: 21b; Losely
Pavel/Shutterstock: 27br; Bill Pugliano/Getty Images: 21t; Riser/Getty Images: 25;
Howard Sandler/Shutterstock: 24b; Vivek Sharma/Alamy: 7;
Mike Sonnenburg/istockphoto: 9cl; Rizwan Tabassum/AFP/Getty Images: 26b;
World Religions PL: front cover, 3, 16b, 19t, 20, 23t; World religions PL/Alamy: 8.
Lisa F. Young/Shutterstock: 10.

Every attempt has been made to clear copyright.
Should there be any inadvertent omission,
please apply to the publisher for rectification.

Printed in Malaysia
Franklin Watts is a division of Hachette Children's Books,
an Hachette UK company.
www.hachette.co.uk

Contents

Why do we celebrate?

We celebrate to mark important events in our lives. We usually share celebrations with people who care about us.

What do you celebrate in your family?

All religions have festivals or holy days. These special days celebrate important events in a religion.

Some people celebrate holy days at home.

Other people celebrate by going to special services at their place of worship.

Do you think it is important to celebrate special events?

How do people get ready for celebrations?
Turn the page to find out...

Getting ready

Some people get ready for religious festivals by decorating their homes and places of worship.

Hindus often use coloured rice flour to draw rangoli patterns on their doorsteps. At the festival of Divali, these welcome the goddess Lakshmi. She brings good luck and blessings.

How do you decorate your home for different celebrations?

At Christmas, Christians celebrate the birth of Jesus Christ, the son of God. The decorations Christians put in homes and churches have special meanings.

God sent an angel to tell Mary she was to be the mother of Jesus.

The Three Wise Men followed a star to find the new baby Jesus.

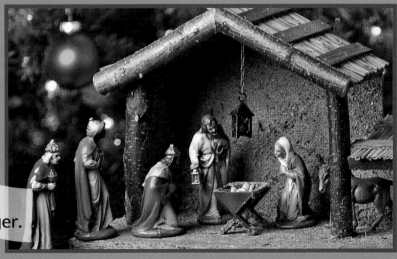

Baby Jesus was born in a stable and slept in a manger.

Talk about...
...how places look when they are decorated for a celebration. Use these words to help you:
- sparkly
- colourful
- special
- shining
- important
- pretty

Special foods

People often cook and eat special foods for celebrations.

Challah bread is special bread that is eaten on the Sabbath, or Jewish day of rest and worship, every week.

What foods do you eat for special days?
What makes them special?

Sometimes people fast (go without food) to remember important events.

At Ramadan, Muslims fast during the day for a month. Afterwards, they feast for three days at the festival of Id-ul-Fitr.

At Lent, Christians remember how Jesus spent 40 days in a desert fasting. In the past, people gave up butter, meat and eggs. On the day before Lent, people made pancakes to use up their butter and eggs.

What other ways do people celebrate religious festivals? Turn the page to find out.

Music and dance

Many religions celebrate with music and song.

Baisakhi is the Sikh New Year. Musicians play songs on the harmonium and tablas (drums). The words of the songs come from the Sikh holy book, the Guru Granth Sahib.

Christian people sing songs called carols at Christmas. The words tell stories about Jesus and the time when he was born.

Which songs have words that are special to you?

Navratri is a Hindu festival of worship and dance.
Some Hindus celebrate Navratri with a special stick dance.

How do you show you are happy when you celebrate?

Talk about...
...how singing together makes people feel.
You could use words like: •happiness •sharing
•belonging •togetherness

Dressing up

People dress up in different ways for different celebrations.

In Tibet, monks dress up in colourful costumes for the Buddhist New Year festival. They do a special dance to frighten away any evil from the previous year.

What do you wear for special days and celebrations?

Talk about...

...why we wear special clothes for celebrations. How do clothes help to make a celebration special? Think about what they show other people.

Wedding services are important celebrations.
Everyone dresses up for weddings.

Christian brides in
some countries wear
white dresses.

Sikh grooms often wear
a red or pink turban.
Sikh brides wear red,
orange or pink dresses.
For Sikhs, red is a
lucky colour!

Giving gifts

People often give gifts on special days.

Raksha Bandhan celebrates the love between Hindu brothers and sisters. Sisters put red and gold threads around their brothers' wrists. Brothers give sisters presents or money.

How does it make you feel to give gifts?

Christians believe God gave Jesus as a gift to the world. That is why Christians give gifts to each other at Christmas.

Muslims give gifts of money at the festival of Id-ul-Fitr. The money is shared out among poor people, so that everyone can celebrate the festival.

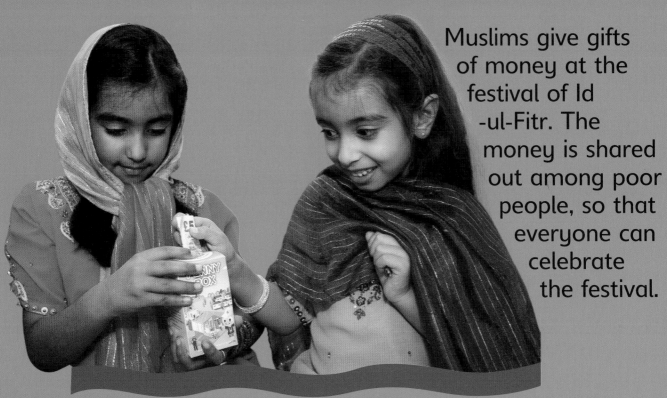

Acting out stories

In some festivals, people act out important stories from their religion.

At the festival of Dassera, Hindus act the story of the god Rama. He rescued his wife Sita from the ten-headed demon king Ravana. The story teaches that good wins over evil.

Have you acted in any plays?
What did the plays teach people?

At the Jewish festival of Purim, children dress up and act out the story of Esther. Esther stopped a wicked man called Haman from killing Jews in Persia 2,000 years ago.

In nativity plays at Christmas, Christian children tell the story of when Jesus was born in a stable.

Why do you think people act out religious stories like this?

How else do celebrations help people to remember the past?
Turn the page to find out.

Remembering the past

Some celebrations remember an important event in the past. Some of these celebrations are happy.

At the Hindu festival of Holi, people throw coloured powder at each other. This reminds them of Krishna, a god who loved to play tricks when he was a boy.

What is a happy time of year for you?
How do you celebrate?

Some festivals are serious. They remind people of important events.

During Passover, Jewish people remember when Jews escaped from slavery in Egypt. God sent ten terrible disasters that killed Egyptians but 'passed over' the Jews.

On Good Friday, Christians remember how Jesus died. Good Friday services are sad. On Easter Sunday services recall how Jesus came back to life.

Which festivals remember important people?
Turn the page to find out.

Remembering people

Some religious festivals remember important people.

In Sri Lanka, Wesak celebrations remember
Buddha's birthday with a flower festival. Flowers
are beautiful and smell good, but they wilt and die.
This reminds Buddhists of Buddha's teaching that
nothing lasts for ever.

Sikhs celebrate the birth of Guru Nanak. He was the founder of Sikhism. Sikhs read the Sikh holy book from beginning to end.

Some Muslims remember the birthday of the Prophet Muhammad. People celebrate by telling stories about the Prophet's life. In some countries, streets and mosques are lit up.

Talk about...
...how these celebrations are the same and how they are different. Think about what people are celebrating and how they celebrate.

Which celebrations give thanks to God?
Turn the page to find out.

Festivals of thanks

At harvest festivals, people thank God for food grown on the land.

The Christian harvest festival reminds Christians of the good things God gives them. People bring gifts of food to church to give to people in need.

For the Sukkot harvest festival, some Jews build a garden hut. This reminds them of when God provided for Jewish people in the wilderness long ago.

What are the similarities and differences between these two festivals?

Some celebrations are about being thankful to other people.

Children often give their mothers a gift and a card on Mothering Sunday.

In church, Christians may pray for mothers and families. Some have special family services for the whole family.

Are there times in your life when you need to say thank you?
How do you make saying thank you special?

Finding festivals

There are clues about festivals all around us. Look for decorations, displays, cards and gifts, or special food for sale.

a.

b.

Which festivals can you see evidence for in these pictures? The answers are at the bottom of page 27.

 c.

 d.

Answers:
a = Holi
b = Raksha Bandhan
c = Christmas
d = Easter

The six main faiths

The world's six main faiths are Hinduism, Islam, Christianity, Sikhism, Buddhism and Judaism. Each of the six main faiths have different beliefs:

Hindus believe there is one God that can take different forms. Hindus worship these different gods and goddesses.

Christians believe there is one God who has three parts: The Father, the Son and the Holy Spirit. Jesus is the son of God and was sent to Earth to save people.

Buddhists do not worship a God. They follow the teachings of a man called Buddha and try to live in the way he taught.

Muslims follow the religion of Islam. They follow five rules known as the Five Pillars: to believe in one God – Allah, to pray five times a day, to fast during the month of Ramadan, to give money to the poor and to go on pilgrimage to Makkah.

Jewish people believe that there is one God who made everything and that they should follow Jewish law.

Sikhs believe that there is one God who made everything. They follow the teachings of ten Gurus (teachers) who told people what God wanted.

Useful words

Disasters – terrible events, such as fires or floods, that cause a lot of damage.

Event – something that happens. An event is usually something important that happens.

Evidence – facts, objects and other things that tell you something is true.

Fast – to eat little or no food. Muslims fast in the day during Ramadan, and eat at night.

Harmonium – a musical instrument that is like a small keyboard.

Harvest – the time of year when farmers pick or dig up many crops (foods from plants).

Holy book – important book that has teachings or stories about a religion.

Pray – to speak to, give thanks to or ask for help from God.

Prophet – a person sent by God to give people messages from God and tell them about God's teachings.

Religion – belief in a God or gods. Islam and Christianity are two religions.

Slavery – when one person is owned by another. Slaves are forced to work for other people without pay and are often treated badly.

Worship – to show respect or love for God or gods. Some people worship by praying and singing.

Index

About this book

Ways into RE is designed to develop children's knowledge of the world's main religions and to help them respect different religions, beliefs, values and traditions and understand how they influence society and the world. This title 'Celebrations' is a way in for children to draw on their experience of special days, and relate it to different religions.

• The children could discuss why we need celebrations (pages 6–7). Are they just for fun and presents? Or do they make us stop and think about important events or people who are important to us?

• Symbols are important to most festivals, whether they are foods, decorations, clothes or gestures. To help the children understand the importance of symbolism in decorations and foods (pages 8–11), they could make some. For example, they could make ladder bread or Indian burfi, sweets people eat at Divali, or decorations such as Christmas stars. When talking about fasting, they could also research why Muslims fast during Ramadan.

• Stories are important ways to learn about festivals. Children could read the story behind a festival and then act it out with puppets, or themselves.

• Children could discuss and think about the idea of gifts, about how giving and receiving gifts makes them feel, about the fact that gifts that cost nothing can make people happy (see pages 16–17). This could lead to discussions about Jesus as a gift from God and why giving gifts often has special meaning. What gifts are really important or valuable?

• Children could discuss the wider use of colour symbols in the world, for example, red as a warning colour in some countries (red traffic light). They could think about the way different colours have different meanings, depending on where you are. For example, white would not be worn in a Sikh wedding because for Sikhs white is an unlucky colour!

• Many celebrations are about remembering or thanking particular people (pages 22–25). The children could think about someone they should thank, and write thank you letters.

• You could provide a selection of objects from different festivals. Children could work together to label them with the festival to which they belong (pages 26–27).